ANIMALS OF THE BIBLE

"From the LION to the SNAIL"

By: **Dr. David Darom**

Photographs: **Yossi Eshbol**

Photo credits:

All photographs © Yossi Eshbol unless otherwise stated.

Photographs © Dr. David Darom:	Cow; Sheep; Camel; Goat; Chameleon; Crocodile's Jaw; Fish in the Sea; Fish; Scorpion; Spider; Cicada; Cricket; Grasshopper; Pestilence; Gnat; Flies; Silkworm; Ant; Locust; Blue; Purple; Snail; Frog Fossil; Judean Desert.
Photograph © Nir Darom:	Raven.
Photographs © Pinhas Amitai:	Dog; Cock; Peacock; Millipede; Honey Bee; Moth.

© All rights reserved by Palphot Ltd.

No part of this publication may be reproduced, stored in any retrievable system or transmitted in any form or by any means, electronic, mechanical, photocopying, recording or otherwise without prior written permission by the Publisher.

Printed by Israphot.
Designed by F. Klevitsky

Produced by Palphot Ltd., P.O.Box 2, Herzlia 46100, Israel.
Tel: 09-9525252, Fax: 09-9525277, e-mail: palphot@inter.net.il
www.palphot.com
ISBN 965-280-106-2

PUBLISHED BY PALPHOT LTD.

Introduction

The various animals mentioned in the Bible were in most cases associated with the fauna existing in the Holy Land and its neighboring countries at the time, over 2000 years ago. Only a handful of species noted in the scriptures were imported through trading with other kingdoms, mainly from Africa and Asia.

Not all species mentioned in the Bible survived through the ages in these parts of the world, although several of the larger mammals such as bears (I Samuel 17:34-35), were still encountered in the early 20th century; lions do not roam the mountains and deserts of Israel anymore; Roe deer and Fallow deer (Deer and Roebuck, Deuteronomy 14:4-6) were hunted to extinction in the early 20th century. Leopards, on the other hand, have recently been sighted in the Judean Desert.

This book quotes the New Revised Standard Version (NRSV) of the Bible. Several of the animal species were not easy to identify and some of them even received different names in the various English translations. At times, the original Hebrew version had to be consulted in order to decide on the final identification. Even so things were not always simple and conclusive, forcing the author to leave some of the most speculative and controversial references for a more extensive study.

In one case, Jeremiah 8:7, the King James Version (KJV) mentions one of the birds as a "swallow", as does the New Revised Standard Version. In Hebrew we find the same bird as a "Sis" which indicates a Swift. The Hebrew version is also zoologically correct since only the swifts "...*observe the time of their coming*" being a migratory bird in the Holy Land.

Another such example can be found in Isaiah 13:21. Here the King James Version mentions one of the birds as being "doleful creatures", and the NRSV calls them "howling creatures". In Hebrew we find the same bird as "Ohim". Since the word "Oah" in Hebrew stands for an Eagle Owl, a bird known to howl at night in desolate places, this should be considered a reasonably correct identification.

The Prophets spoke to people living on their land surrounded by conspicuous plants and animal life. Many of the metaphors used were therefore related to common animals, wild as well as domestic, known to all the listeners. As in the words of Isaiah: "*The wolf shall live with the lamb, the leopard shall lie down with the kid, the calf and the lion and the fatling together, and a little child shall lead them*" (Isaiah 11:6). Thus the speaker was able to illustrate points in his speech in a manner understandable even to the most illiterate crowds.

Today the majority of Bible readers are able to comprehend these analogies even without clearly identifying the exact species involved. A clear identification of the animals concerned would surely enhance one's understanding and appreciation of the script.

Regretfully, not much has recently been published in writing on the animals mentioned in the Bible. Hopefully this publication will inspire others to do more comprehensive studies, leaving no stone unturned and cross-referring to the zoogeography of the region and various archeological findings of both human artifacts as well as animal remains. ∎

ANIMALS of

And God said, "Let the waters bring forth swarms of living creatures, and let birds fly above the earth across the dome of the sky." So God created the great sea monsters and every living creature that moves, of every kind, with which the waters swarm, and every winged bird of every kind. And God saw that it was good. God blessed them, saying, "Be fruitful and multiply and fill the waters in the seas, and let birds multiply on the earth." And there was evening and there was morning, the fifth day. And God said, "Let the earth bring forth living creatures of every kind: cattle and creeping things and wild animals of the earth of every kind." And it was so.
(Genesis 1:20-25)

And of every living thing, of all flesh, you shall bring two of every kind into the ark, to keep them alive with you; they shall be male and female. Of the birds according to their kinds, and of the animals according to their kinds, of every creeping thing of the ground according to its kind, two of every kind shall come in to you, to keep them alive ... Two and two, male and female, went into the ark with Noah, as God had commanded Noah ... They went into the ark with Noah, two and two of all flesh in which there was the breath of life.
(Genesis 6:19 - 7:16)

LION

FOX

CAMEL

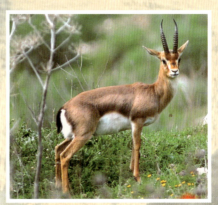
GAZELLE

the BIBLE

Animals in the Bible are distinctly classified into those fit to be eaten and those unfit for human consumption:

"The LORD spoke to Moses and Aaron, saying to them: Speak to the people of Israel, saying: From among all the land animals, these are the creatures that you may eat. Any animal that has divided hoofs and is cleft-footed and chews the cud, such you may eat. But among those that chew the cud or have divided hoofs, you shall not ea the following: the camel, for even though it chews the cud, it does not have divided hoofs; it is unclean for you."

(Lev.11:1-4)

The writers of the Bible often used common qualities found in different animals to illustrate or symbolize a variety of qualities and powers:

"I looked up and saw a ram standing beside the river. It had two horns. Both horns were long, but one was longer than the other, and the longer one came up second. I saw the ram charging westward and northward and southward. All beasts were powerless to withstand it, and no one could rescue its power; it did as it pleased and became strong. As I was watching, a male goat appeared from the west, coming across the face of the whole earth without touching the ground. The goat had a horn between its eyes. As for the ram that you saw with the two horns, these are the kings of Media and Persia The male goat is the king of Greece, and the great horn between its eyes is the first king. As for the horn that was broken, in place of which four others arose, four kingdoms shall arise from his nation, but not with his power."

(Daniel 8:3-22)

PURPLE

LIZARD

FROG

SEA GULL

FISH

5

1. Vertebrates

LION (Lion) *Panthera leo*

In biblical times lions roamed the desert. Surviving in the region till medieval days, they were often encountered by shepherds and travelers. In some cases lions were set upon men as a death penalty. Lions stand for courage and are often mentioned in reference to strength and boldness.

*Judah is a **lion's** whelp; from the prey, my son, you have gone up. He crouches down, he stretches out like a lion, like a lioness— who dares rouse him up?*
Genesis 49:9

*The **lion**, which is mightiest among wild animals and does not turn back before any;*
Proverbs 30:30

*The **lion** has roared; who will not fear? The Lord GOD has spoken; who can but prophesy?*
Amos 3:8

IVORY (Elephant) *Loxodonta africana*

*For the king had a fleet of ships of Tarshish at sea with the fleet of Hiram. Once every three years the fleet of ships of Tarshish used to come bringing gold, silver, **ivory**, apes, and peacocks.*
1 Kings 10:22

*The Rhodians traded with you; many coastlands were your own special markets; they brought you in payment **ivory tusks** and ebony.*
Ezekiel 27:15

APE (Ape) *Simioidea*

*For the king had a fleet of ships of Tarshish at sea with the fleet of Hiram. Once every three years the fleet of ships of Tarshish used to come bringing gold, silver, ivory, **apes**, and peacocks.*

1 Kings 10:22

LEOPARD (Leopard) *Panthera pardus*

The leopard was quite common in biblical Israel and has reappeared recently in the Judean Desert.

*The wolf shall live with the lamb, the **leopard** shall lie down with the kid, the calf and the lion and the fatling together, and a little child shall lead them.*

Isaiah 11:6

*Can Ethiopians change their skin or **leopards** their spots? Then also you can do good who are accustomed to do evil.*

Jeremiah 13:23

HYENA (Striped Hyena) *Hayaena hayaena*

A carrion eating mammal, falling between the feline and canine families, known for its disturbing howling.

Hyenas will cry in its towers, and jackals in the pleasant palaces; its time is close at hand, and its days will not be prolonged.
Isaiah 13:22

*Another company turned toward Beth-horon, and another company turned toward the mountain that looks down upon the valley of **Zeboim** toward the wilderness.*
1 Samuel 13:18

BEAR (Syrian Bear) *Ursus arctos syriacus*

The Syrian brown bear was indigenous to the land of the bible until the early 20th century. Known as a carnivore it also feeds on fruits, vegetables and insects. Generally considered harmless to people, a bear can become dangerous when it or its young are threatened or provoked.

*But David said to Saul, "Your servant used to keep sheep for his father; and whenever a lion or a **bear** came, and took a lamb from the flock, I went after it and struck it down, rescuing the lamb from its mouth; and if it turned against me, I would catch it by the jaw, strike it down, and kill it.*
1 Samuel 17:34-35

*When he turned around and saw them, he cursed them in the name of the LORD. Then two **she-bears** came out of the woods and mauled forty-two of the boys.*
2 Kings 2:24

WOLF (Wolf) *Canis lupus*

*Benjamin is a ravenous **wolf**, in the morning devouring the prey, and at evening dividing the spoil.*
Genesis 49:27

*The **wolf** and the lamb shall feed together, and the lion shall eat straw like the bullock: and dust shall be the serpent's meat. They shall not hurt nor destroy in all my holy mountain, saith the LORD.*
Isaiah 65:25

FOX (Fox) *Vulpes vulpes*

The fox is distinguished by its pointed face, large and erect triangular ears, and its bushy tail. Known for its craftiness mainly in eluding its enemies, it feeds mostly on insects, rodents various other small animals and birds as well as on fruits.

*So Samson went and caught three hundred **foxes**, and took some torches; and he turned the foxes tail to tail, and put a torch between each pair of tails. When he had set fire to the torches, he let the foxes go into the standing grain of the Philistines, and burned up the shocks and the standing grain, as well as the vineyards and olive groves.*
Judges 15:4

*Catch us the **foxes**, the little **foxes**, that ruin the vineyards– for our vineyards are in blossom.*
Song of Songs 2:15

*And Jesus said to him, "**Foxes** have holes, and birds of the air have nests; but the Son of Man has nowhere to lay his head."*
Luke 9:58

JACKAL (Jackal) *Canis aureus*

The jackal resembles a wolf but is smaller and has a shorter tail. Common in biblical Israel, it travels in packs and feeds on carrion as well as freshly killed prey.

*The burning sand shall become a pool, and the thirsty ground springs of water; the haunt of **jackals** shall become a swamp, the grass shall become reeds and rushes.*
Isaiah 35:7

*Hear, a noise! Listen, it is coming– a great commotion from the land of the north to make the cities of Judah a desolation, a lair of **jackals**.*
Jeremiah 10:22

DOG (Dog) *Canis lupus familiaris*

*You shall be people consecrated to me; therefore you shall not eat any meat that is mangled by beasts in the field; you shall throw it to the **dogs**.*
Exodus 22:31

*For to him that is joined to all the living there is hope: for a living **dog** is better than a dead lion.*
Ecclesiastes 9:4

In ancient times dogs were not kept as pets . In the bible they are usually mentioned unfavorably, being unattractive scavengers.

10

BEHEMOTH (Hippopotamus) *Hippopotamus amphibus*

*Look at **Behemoth**, which I made just as I made you; it eats grass like an ox. Its strength is in its loins, and its power in the muscles of its belly.*
Job 40:15-16

HORSE (Arabian Horse) *Equus caballus orientalis*

*The Egyptians pursued them, all Pharaoh's **horses** and chariots, his chariot drivers and his army;*
Exodus 14:9

*Then took Haman the apparel and the **horse**, and arrayed Mordecai, and brought him on horseback through the street of the city, and proclaimed before him, Thus shall it be done unto the man whom the king delighteth to honour.*
Esther 6:11

Horses were from ancient times closely associated with man. They were used for domestic chores as well as being a formidable part of an effective fighting force. In the Bible horses also have an illustrative role, at times representing glorious victories or, elsewhere, the impetuous manner of dashing into battle regardless of the consequences.

DONKEY (Donkey) *Equus asinus*

Donkeys were common in Biblical times, used mainly for riding and carrying heavy loads in arid zones and over rough terrain. Sure-footed, steady going and needing simple care, donkeys were a popular choice with the less wealthy people who could not afford the larger, expensive horses or mules.

*So Moses took his wife and his sons, put them on a **donkey** and went back to the land of Egypt.*
Exodus 4:20

*Rejoice greatly, O daughter Zion! Shout aloud, O daughter Jerusalem! Lo, your king comes to you; triumphant and victorious is he, humble and riding on a donkey, on a colt, the foal of a **donkey**.*
Zechariah 9:9

CAMEL (Camel) *Camelus dromedarius*

*Then the servant took ten of his master's **camels** and departed, taking all kinds of choice gifts from his master; and he set out and went to Aram-naharaim, to the city of Nahor.*
Genesis 24:10

*It is easier for a **camel** to go through the eye of a needle, than for a rich man to enter into the kingdom of God.*
Mark 10:25

BULL, COW (Bull, Cow) *Bos taurus*

Wild cattle was found in the Middle East thousands of years ago, surviving the extensive hunting only through domestication.

*Their **bull** gendereth, and faileth not; their cow calveth, and casteth not her calf.*
Job 21:10

*Thy sons have fainted, they lie at the head of all the streets, as a wild **bull** in a net: they are full of the fury of the LORD, the rebuke of thy God.*
Isaiah 51:20

SHEEP (Fat-tailed Sheep) *Ovis orientalis platyura*
RAM (Fat-tailed Sheep) *Ovis orientalis platyura*

Broad-tailed sheep are considered one of the main domestic animals of pastoral life in the Holy Land. Ranging in color from creamy-white to brown, domestic sheep are helpless without their shepherd, soon getting lost and becoming easy prey to wild beasts. Sheep provide their owners with meat, wool, sheepskins, horns (to make sounding horns) and from the earliest times were offered as sacrifices. Figuratively, "sheep" are often used to denoted innocence and defenselessness.

*You shall do the same with your oxen and with your **sheep**: seven days it shall remain with its mother; on the eighth day you shall give it to me.*
Exodus 22:30

*And Aaron and his sons shall eat the flesh of the **ram** and the bread that is in the basket, at the entrance of the tent of meeting.*
Exodus 29:32

*And Abraham lifted up his eyes, and looked, and behold behind him a **ram** caught in a thicket by his horns: and Abraham went and took the ram, and offered him up for a burnt offering in the stead of his son.*
Genesis 22:13

13

GOAT (Member Goat) *Capra hircus mambrica*

*Then Aaron shall lay both his hands on the head of the live **goat**, and confess over it all the iniquities of the people of Israel, and all their transgressions, all their sins, putting them on the head of the goat, and sending it away into the wilderness by means of someone designated for the task. The goat shall bear on itself all their iniquities to a barren region; and the goat shall be set free in the wilderness.*

Leviticus 16:21

*For seven days you shall provide daily a **goat** for a sin offering; also a bull and a ram from the flock, without blemish, shall be provided.*

Ezekiel 43:25

DEER (Roe Deer) *Capreolus capreolus*
GAZELLE (Mountain Gazelle) *Gazella gazella*
ROEBUCK (Fallow deer) *Dama dama*
IBEX (Nubian Ibex) *Capra Ibex*
ANTELOPE (Arabian Oryx) *Oryx leucoryx*

DEER (Roe Deer) *Capreolus capreolus*

GAZELLE (Mountain Gazelle) *Gazella gazella*

15

ROEBUCK (Fallow deer) *Dama dama*

*These are the animals you may eat: the ox, the sheep, the goat, the **deer**, the **gazelle**, the **roebuck**, the wild goat, the **ibex**, the **antelope**, and the mountain-sheep. Any animal that divides the hoof and has the hoof cleft in two, and chews the cud, among the animals, you may eat.*

Deuteronomy 14:4-6

IBEX (Nubian Ibex) *Capra ibex*

ANTELOPE (Arabian Oryx) *Oryx leucoryx*

PIG; BOAR (Wild Boar) *Sus scrofa*

Pigs were ruled unacceptable for food or sacrifice since they are not cud-chewers. The Jewish tradition viewed the swine as an especially loathsome creature. It was therefore used to describe a most inappropriate situation, when comparing a beautiful but stupid woman to a pig with a gold nose-ring.

*The **pig**, for even though it has divided hoofs and is cleft-footed, it does not chew the cud; it is unclean for you.*
Leviticus 11:8

*The **boar** from the forest ravages it, and all that move in the field feed on it.*
Psalms 80:13

*Like a gold ring in a **pig's** snout is a beautiful woman without good sense.*
Proverbs 11:22

*So he went and hired himself out to one of the citizens of that country, who sent him to his fields to feed the **pigs**.*
Luke 15:15

HARE (Brown Hare) *Lepus capensis*

*But among those that chew the cud or have divided hoofs, you shall not eat ...The **hare**, for even though it chews the cud, it does not have divided hoofs; it is unclean for you.*
Leviticus 11:4-7

BADGER; CONEY (Syrian Rock Hyrax)
Procovia capensis

A small rabbit-like mammal that lives in crags or rocks. It is considered unclean for consumption by the Israelites.

*But among those that chew the cud or have divided hoofs, you shall not eat the following ... The rock **badger**, for even though it chews the cud, it does not have divided hoofs; it is unclean for you.*
Leviticus 11:4-5

*The **badgers** are a people without power, yet they make their homes in the rocks;*
Proverbs 30:26

*The high mountains are for the wild goats; the rocks are a refuge for the **coneys**.*
Psalms 104:18

MOUSE (House Mouse) *Mus musculus*

*These are unclean for you among the creatures that swarm upon the earth: the weasel, the **mouse** ...*
Leviticus 11:29-30

18

EAGLE (Griffon Vulture) *Gyps fulvus*

EAGLE (Griffon Vulture) *Gyps fulvus*

*Three things are too wonderful for me; four I do not understand: the way of an **eagle** in the sky, the way of a snake on a rock, the way of a ship on the high seas, and the way of a man with a girl.*
Proverbs 30:18-19

*As an **eagle** stirs up its nest, and hovers over its young; as it spreads its wings, takes them up, and bears them aloft on its pinions.*
Deuteronomy 32:11

*You have seen what I did to the Egyptians, and how I bore you on **eagles'** wings and brought you to myself.*
Exodus 19:4

Being a large, swift and powerful bird of prey, the eagle is often mentioned in the Bible in a figurative manner. In the words of the prophets, it symbolizes the warring forces of enemy armies in their forceful and unexpected attacks. Eagles often characterize Babylonian and Egyptian rulers and are referred to as the creatures attending God's throne in readiness to announce His judgment.

VULTURE (Lappet-Faced Vulture) *Torgos tracheliotus*

19

BUZZARD (Honey Buzzard) *Pernis apivorus*
KITE (Black Kite) *Milvus migrans*
NIGHTHAWK (Kestrel) *Falco tinnunculus*
SEA GULL (Gull) *Larus ridibundus*
HAWK (Sparrow Hawk) *Accipiter nisus*
VULTURE (Lappet-Faced Vulture) *Torgos tracheliotus*

The fifth day of creation brought into being both the birds and creatures of the sea. Identification of the many birds mentioned nearly 300 times in the Bible is not an easy matter. Their habits, the context in which they are mentioned and knowledge of the species common to the region should all be considered before trying to make any kind of decision. Birds are often used in the Bible as symbols, adapting figuratively some of their commonly known qualities and natural habits. Birds of prey symbolize aggression as opposed to the peaceful domestic fowl or the wandering characteristics of migratory birds.

VULTURE (Lappet-Faced Vulture) *Torgos tracheliotus*   **KITE** (Black Kite) *Milvus migrans*

20

NIGHTHAWK (Kestrel) *Falco tinnunculus*

*These you shall regard as detestable among the birds. They shall not be eaten; they are an abomination: the eagle, the vulture, the **osprey**, the **buzzard**, the **kite** of any kind; every raven of any kind; the ostrich, the **nighthawk**, the **sea gull**, the **hawk** of any kind; the **little owl**, the cormorant, the great owl, the water hen, the desert owl, the **carrion vulture**, the stork, the **heron** of any kind, the **hoopoe**, and the bat.*

Leviticus 11:13-19

SEA GULL (Black Headed Gull) *Larus ridibundus*

HAWK (Sparrow Hawk) *Accipiter nisus*

LITTLE OWL (Little Owl) *Athene noctua*
CARRION VULTURE (Egyptian Vulture) *Neophron perenopterus*
HERON (Grey Heron) *Ardea cinera*
HOOPOE (Hoopoe) *Upupa epops*

LITTLE OWL (Little Owl) *Athene noctua*

CARRION VULTURE (Egyptian Vulture)

HERON (Grey Heron) *Ardea cinera*

HOOPOE (Hoopoe) *Upupa epops*

OSTRICH (Ostrich) *Struthio camelus*

*These you shall regard as detestable among the birds... the **ostrich**...*
Leviticus 11:13-19

*The **ostrich**'s wings flap wildly, though its pinions lack plumage. For it leaves its eggs to the earth, and lets them be warmed on the ground, forgetting that a foot may crush them, and that a wild animal may trample them.*
Job 39:13

PEACOCK (Common Peafowl) *Pavo cristatus*

*For the king had a fleet of ships of Tarshish at sea with the fleet of Hiram. Once every three years the fleet of ships of Tarshish used to come bringing gold, silver, ivory, apes, and **peacocks**.*
1 Kings 10:22

STORK (Stork) *Ciconia ciconia*
CRANE (Crane) *Grus grus*

STORK (Stork) *Ciconia ciconia*

*Even the **stork** in the heavens knows its times; and the turtledove, swallow, and **crane** observe the time of their coming; but my people do not know the ordinance of the LORD.*

Jeremiah 8:7

CRANE (Crane) *Grus grus*

*The trees of the LORD are watered abundantly, the cedars of Lebanon that he planted. In them the birds build their nests; the **stork** has its home in the fir trees.*

Psalms 104:16-17

OWL (Long Eared Owl) *Asio otus*

*But the hawk and the hedgehog shall possess it; the **owl** and the raven shall live in it. He shall stretch the line of confusion over it, and the plummet of chaos over its nobles.*

Isaiah 34:11

24

HOWLING CREATURES (Eagle Owl) *Bubo bubo*

*But wild animals will lie down there, and its houses will be full of **howling creatures**; there ostriches will live, and there goat-demons will dance.*
Isaiah 13:21

RAVEN (Raven) *Corvus corone*

*At the end of forty days Noah opened the window of the ark that he had made and sent out the **raven**; and it went to and fro until the waters were dried up from the earth.*
Genesis 8:7

*His head is as the most fine gold, his locks are bushy, and black as a **raven**.*
Song of Songs 5:11

The first bird mentioned by name in the Bible, the raven is considered to be one of the most adaptable and resourceful of all birds. The known flying strength of the raven as well as its ability to survive on a variety of food, made it an apt candidate for being the first creature to be sent outside the ark as the waters began to recede.

SPARROW (House Sparrow) *Passer domesticus*

*Like a **sparrow** in its flitting, like a swallow in its flying, an undeserved curse goes nowhere.*
Proverbs 26:2

TURTLEDOVE (Turtle Dove) *Streptolepia turtur*
PIGEON (Rock Dove) *Columba livia*

TURTLEDOVE (Turtle Dove) *Streptolepia turtur*

*The flowers appear on the earth; the time of singing has come, and the voice of the **turtledove** is heard in our land.*
Song of Songs 2:12

*On the eighth day they shall bring two **turtledoves** or two young **pigeons** to the priest at the entrance of the tent of meeting.*
Numbers 6:10

*Who are these that fly like a cloud, and like **doves** to their windows?*
Isaiah 60:8

PIGEON (Rock Dove) *Columba livia*

26

COCK; HEN (Rooster; Hen) *Gallus gallus*

*Therefore, keep awake - for you do not know when the master of the house will come, in the evening, or at midnight, or at **cockcrow**, or at dawn.*
Mark 13:35

*"Jerusalem, Jerusalem, the city that kills the prophets and stones those who are sent to it! How often have I desired to gather your children together as a **hen** gathers her brood under her wings, and you were not willing!"*
Matthew 23:37

QUAIL (Quail) *Coturnix coturnix*

*Then a wind went out from the LORD, and it brought **quails** from the sea and let them fall beside the camp, about a day's journey on this side and a day's journey on the other side, all around the camp.*
Numbers 11:31

The common migratory quail moves northward in spring from within Africa passing Egypt and the Holy Land. They travel in large flocks, migrating by stages and often landing in a state of exhaustion, becoming easy to catch.

GECKO (Gecko) *Hemidactylus turcicus*
LIZARD (Lizard) *Lacerta trilineata*
SAND LIZARD (Skink) *Calcides; Scincus*
CHAMELEON (Chameleon) *Chamaeleo chamaeleon*

GECKO (Gecko) *Hemidactylus turcicus*

LIZARD (Lizard) *Lacerta trilineata*

Lizards are small four-legged reptiles with long tails and scaly skin. More than 40 kinds are found in the Holy Land.

> *These are unclean for you among the creatures that swarm upon the earth: ...the great **lizard** according to its kind, the **gecko**, ...the lizard the **sand lizard**, and the **chameleon**.*
> *Leviticus 11:29-30*

> *The **lizard** can be grasped in the hand, yet it is found in kings' palaces.*
> *Proverbs 30:28*

SAND LIZARD (Skink) *Calcides; Scincus*

CHAMELEON (Chameleon) *Chamaeleo chamaeleon*

The chameleon is quite common in the Holy Land, but is rarely seen because of its incredible ability to change color and disguise itself against the background. Usually moving very slowly, this tree dwelling lizard approaches its prey, usually small insects, catching them from a distance with its accurately aimed sticky tongue.

SERPENT, ADDER (Palestinian Viper)
Vipera palaestinae

*Now the **serpent** was more subtle than any other wild creature that the Lord God had made.*

Genesis 3:1

*Then the LORD sent poisonous **serpents** among the people, and they bit the people, so that many Israelites died.*

Numbers 21:6

VIPER (Cerastes Viper) *Cerastes cerastes*

*Dan shall be a snake by the roadside, a **viper** along the path, that bites the horse's heels so that its rider falls backward.*

Genesis 49:17

*Do not look at wine when it is red, when it sparkles in the cup and goes down smoothly. At the last it bites like a serpent, and stings like an **adder**.*

Proverbs 23:31-32

ASP (Egyptian Cobra) *Walterinnesia aegyptia*

*...their wine is the poison of serpents, the cruel venom of **asps**.*
Deuteronomy 32:33

SNAKE (Crocodile) *Crocodilus niloticus*

"*When Pharaoh says to you, 'Perform a wonder,' then you shall say to Aaron, 'Take your staff and throw it down before Pharaoh, and it will become a **snake**.'*"
Exodus 7:9

The last specimen of a living crocodile was caught in the Holy Land in 1917 by a British soldier. Part of the lower jaw, seen here, was photographed at the Hebrew University of Jerusalem where its remains are preserved in the reptile collection.

FROG (Frog) *Rana ridibunda*

*If you refuse to let them go, I will plague your whole country with **frogs**. The river shall swarm with frogs; they shall come up into your palace, into your bedchamber and your bed, and into the houses of your officials and of your people, and into your ovens and your kneading bowls.*
Exodus 8:2-3

FISH (Fish) *Pisces*

God blessed them, and God said to them, "Be fruitful and multiply, and fill the earth and subdue it; and have dominion over the **fish** of the sea and over the birds of the air and over every living thing that moves upon the earth."

Genesis 1:28

We remember the **fish**, which we did eat in Egypt freely; the cucumbers, and the melons, and the leeks, and the onions, and the garlic.

Numbers 11:5

These you may eat, of all that are in the waters. Everything in the waters that has fins and scales, whether in the seas or in the streams... such you may eat. Everything in the waters that does not have fins and scales is detestable to you.

Leviticus 11:9-12

Its **fish** will be of a great many kinds, like the fish of the Great Sea.

Ezekiel 47:10

Now the LORD had prepared a great **fish** to swallow up Jonah. And Jonah was in the belly of the fish three days and three nights.

Jonah 1:17

Jesus asked them, "How many loaves have you?" They said, "Seven, and a few small **fish**." ... he took the seven loaves and the fish; and after giving thanks he broke them and gave them to the disciples, and the disciples gave them to the crowds ... Those who had eaten were four thousand men, besides women and children.

Matthew 15:34-38

Oreochromis aureus

2. Invertebrates

SCORPION (Scorpion) *Leiurus quinquestriatus*

...the LORD your God, who led you through the great and terrible wilderness, an arid wasteland with poisonous snakes and **scorpions**.
Deuteronomy 8:15

And to them it was given that they should not kill them, but that they should be tormented five months: and their torment was as the torment of a **scorpion**, when he striketh a man.
Revelation 9:5

WHATEVER HAS MANY FEET (Millipede)
Graphidostrepus syriacus

All creatures that swarm upon the earth are detestable; they shall not be eaten. Whatever moves on its belly, and whatever moves on all fours, or **whatever has many feet**.
Leviticus 11:41-42

SPIDER (Spider) *Araneae*

*They hatch adders' eggs, and weave the **spider's** web; whoever eats their eggs dies, and the crushed egg hatches out a viper. Their webs cannot serve as clothing; they cannot cover themselves with what they make. Their works are works of iniquity, and deeds of violence are in their hands.*

Isaiah 59:5-6

*Their confidence is gossamer, a **spider's** house their trust.*

Job 8:14

CICADA (Cicada) *Cicadoidea*

*All your trees and the fruit of your ground the **cicada** shall take over.*

Deuteronomy 28:42

At times, even the original Hebrew version of the Bible is extremely vague causing translators to make up their own speculative decisions. In the KJV we find that " All thy trees and fruit of thy land shall the locust consume" (Deut. 28:42). The NRSV gives a more probable translation (Cicada), which seems closer to the Hebrew "tziltzal" indicating an insect that produces a "ringing" sound.

35

PESTILENCE (Wasp) *Vespa orientalis*

*Moreover, the LORD your God will send the **pestilence** against them, until even the survivors and the fugitives are destroyed.*
Deuteronomy 7:20

BEE (Honey Bee) *Apis mellifera*

*The Amorites who lived in that hill country then came out against you and chased you as **bees** do.*
Deuteronomy 1:44

*Then he went down and talked with the woman, and she pleased Samson. After a while he returned to marry her, and he turned aside to see the carcass of the lion, and there was a swarm of **bees** in the body of the lion, and honey.*
Judges 14:7-8

Bees are sometimes mentioned in the Bible in connection with the honey they produce or when the enemies of Israel are likened to bees. Elsewhere, the word honey (" ...milk and honey") refers to sweet date extracts.

GNAT (Mosquito) *Culex; Anopheles*

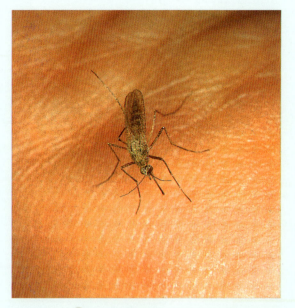

Gnats could be any of a number of tiny two-winged insects, many of which are bloodsuckers, the most common and bothersome being the mosquito.

*And they did so; Aaron stretched out his hand with his staff and struck the dust of the earth, and **gnats** came on humans and animals alike; all the dust of the earth turned into gnats throughout the whole land of Egypt.*
Exodus 8:17

*You blind guides! You strain out a **gnat** but swallow a camel!*
Matthew 23:24

FLY (Flies) *Musca; Lucilia*

Flies are two-winged insects that usually lay their eggs in decayed or waste matter. Having pads of sticky hair on their feet, they carry around large quantities of bacteria thus being a hazard to various food products.

*Dead **flies** make the perfumer's ointment give off a foul odor; so a little folly outweighs wisdom and honor.*
Ecclesiastes 10:1

SILK (Silkworm) *Bombyx mori*

*Cargo of gold, silver, jewels and pearls, fine linen, purple, **silk** and scarlet, all kinds of scented wood, all articles of ivory, all articles of costly wood, bronze, iron, and marble.*
Revelation 18:12

MOTH (Moth) LEPIDOPTERA (Tineola; Tinea)

*For the **moth** will eat them up like a garment, and the worm will eat them like wool; but my deliverance will be forever, and my salvation to all generations.*
Isaiah 51:8

Female clothes moths lay their eggs on fabrics of silk, wool or fir for the emerging destructive caterpillars to feed on.

ANT (Ant) FORMICIDAE (Polyrhachis; Messor)

Go to the ant, you lazybones; consider its ways, and be wise.
Proverbs 6:6
Four things on earth are small, yet they are exceedingly wise: the ants are a people without strength, yet they provide their food in the summer;
Prov. 30:24

LOCUST (Desert Locust) *Shistocerca gregaria*
CRICKET (Katydid) *Tettigonioidea*
GRASSHOPPER (Grasshopper) *Acrididae*

LOCUST (Desert Locust) *Shistocerca gregaria*

Locust are leaping insects related to grasshoppers. Migrating in large swarms they are capable of destroying entire crops and were therefore greatly feared in biblical times. Katydids are also related to grasshoppers, their slender antennas are always longer than their body.

39

All winged insects that walk upon all fours are detestable to you. But among the winged insects that walk on all fours you may eat those that have jointed legs above their feet, with which to leap on the ground. Of them you may eat: the **locust** according to its kind, the bald locust according to its kind, the **cricket** according to its kind, and the **grasshopper** according to its kind.

Leviticus 11:20-22

For they and their livestock would come up, and they would even bring their tents, as thick as **locusts**; neither they nor their camels could be counted; so they wasted the land as they came in.

Judges 6:5

The **locusts** have no king, yet all of them march in rank.

Proverbs 30:27

CRICKET (Katydid) *Tettigonioidea*

GRASSHOPPER (Grasshopper) *Acrididae*

BLUE (Jantina) *Jantina jantina*
PURPLE (Murex) *Bulinus brandaris, Thais haemastoma*

*When they make these sacred vestments for your brother Aaron and his sons to serve me as priests, they shall use gold, **blue, purple**, and crimson yarns, and fine linen.*
Exodus 28:4-5

BLUE (Jantina) *Jantina jantina*

Blue and purple pigments were extracted from several mollusc species found in the shallow coastal waters of the eastern Mediterranean sea. These permanent dyes were extremely valuable since only minute quantities were produced from each creature. They were used mainly to color garments used by priests and wealthy people.

*Speak to the Israelites, and tell them to make fringes on the corners of their garments throughout their generations and to put a **blue** cord on the fringe at each corner.*

Numbers 15:38

*And Mordecai went out from the presence of the king in royal apparel of **blue** and white, and with a great crown of gold, and with a garment of fine linen and **purple**: and the city of Shushan rejoiced and was glad.*

Esther 8:15

PURPLE Thais haemastoma

PURPLE (Murex) Bulinus brandaris

42

SNAIL (Snail) *Helix*

Over one hundred different species of land snails can be found in the region of the Holy Land. Some are northern species while others originate from Africa, possibly brought over by adhering to migrating birds.

*Let them be like the **snail** that dissolves into slime; like the untimely birth that never sees the sun.*

Psalms 58:8

43

ANIMALS of the BIBLE
Alphabetic INDEX

ADDER, SERPENT (Palestinian Viper) *Vipera palaestinae* — Numbers 21:6; Proverbs 23:32

ANT (Ant) **FORMICIDAE** *(Polyrhachis; Messor)* — Proverbs 6:6, 30:24

ANTELOPE (Arabian Oryx) *Oryx Leucoryx* — Deuteronomy 14:4-6

APE (Ape) *Simioidea* — 1 Kings 10:22

ASP (Egyptian Cobra) *Walterinnesia aegyptia* — Deuteronomy 32:33

BADGER; CONEY (Syrian Rock Hyrax) *Procovia capensis* — Psalms 104:18; Proverbs 30:26

BEAR (Syrian Bear) *Ursus arctos syriacus* — 1 Samuel 17:34-35; Isaiah 11:7

BEE (Honey Bee) *Apis mellifera* — Judges 14:7-8

BEHEMOTH (Hippopotamus) *Hippopotamus amphibus* — Job 40:15-16

BLUE (Jantina) *Jantina jantina* — Exodus 28:4-5; Numbers 15:38

BOAR; PIG (Wild Boar) *Sus scrofa* — Leviticus 11:8; Proverbs 11:22

BULL, COW (Bull, Cow) *Bos taurus* — Job 21:10 Isaiah 51:20

BUZZARD (Honey Buzzard) *Pernis apivorus* — Leviticus 11:13-19

CAMEL (Camel) *Camelus dromedarius* — Genesis 24:10; Mark 10:25

CARRION VULTURE (Egyptian Vulture) *Neophron perenopterus* — Leviticus 11:13-19

CHAMELEON (Chameleon) *Chamaeleo chamaeleon* — Leviticus 11:29-30

CICADA (Cicada) *Cicadoidea* — Deuteronomy 28:42

COCK; HEN (Rooster; Hen) *Gallus gallus* — Mark 13:35; Matthew 23:37

CONEY; BADGER (Syrian Rock Hyrax) *Procovia capensis* — Psalms 104:18; Proverbs 30:26

COW, BULL (Cow, Bull) *Bos taurus* — Job 21:10 Isaiah 51:20

CRANE (Crane) *Grus grus* — Jeremiah 8:7

CRICKET (Katydid) *Tettigonioidea* — Leviticus 11:20-22

DEER (Roe Deer) *Capreolus capreolus* — Deuteronomy 14:4-6

DOG (Dog) *Canis familiari* — Exodus 22:31; Ecclesiastes 9:4

DONKEY (Donkey) *Equus asinus* — Exodus 4:20, Zechariah 9:9

EAGLE (Griffon Vulture) *Gyps fulvus* — Exodus 19:4; Leviticus 11:13-19

FISH (Fish) *Pisces* — Leviticus 11:9-12; Numbers 11:5; Ezekiel 47:10, Jonah 1:17

FLY (Flies) *Musca; Lucilia* — Ecclesiastes 10:1

FOX (Fox) *Vulpes vulpes* — Song of Songs 2:15; Judges 15:4

FROG (Frog) *Rana ridibunda* — Exodus 8:2-3

GAZELLE (Mountain Gazelle) *Gazella gazella* — Deuteronomy 14:4-6

GECKO (Gecko) *Hemidactylus turcicus* — Leviticus 11:29-30

GNAT (Mosquito) *Culex; Anopheles* — Exodus 8:17; Matthew 23:24

GOAT (Member Goat) *Capra hircus mambrica* — Deut. 14:4-6; Ezek. 43:25; Lev. 16:21

GRASSHOPPER (Grasshopper) *Acrididae* — Leviticus 11:20-22; Judges 6:5

HARE (Brown Hare) *Lepus capensis* — Leviticus 11:4-7

HAWK (Sparrow Hawk) *Accipiter nisus* — Leviticus 11:13-19; Job 39:26

HEN; COCK (Rooster; Hen) *Gallus gallus* — Mark 13:35; Matthew 23:37

HERON (Grey Heron) *Ardea cinera* — Leviticus 11:13-19

HOOPOE (Hoopoe) *Upupa epops* — Leviticus 11:13-19

Fossilized frog from the Land of the Bible

45

HORSE (Arabian Horse) *Equus caballus orientalis*	Exodus 14:9; Esther 6:11
HOWLING CREATURES (Eagle Owl) *Bubo bubo*	Isaiah 13:21
HYENA (Striped Hyena) *Hayaena hayaena*	1 Samuel 13:18; Isaiah 13:22
IBEX (Nubian Ibex) *Capra ibex*	Deuteronomy 14:4-6
IVORY (Elephant) *Loxodonta africana*	1 Kings. 10:22; Ezekiel 27:15
JACKAL (Jackal) *Canis aureus*	Isaiah 35:7; Jeremiah 10:22
KITE (Black Kite) *Milvus migrans*	Leviticus 11:13-19
LEOPARD (Leopard) *Panthera pardus*	Isaiah 11:6; Jer. 5:6
LION (Lion) *Panthera leo*	Genesis 49:9; Proverbs 30:30
LITTLE OWL (Little Owl) *Athene noctua*	Leviticus 11:13-19
LIZARD (Green Lizard) *Lacerta trilineata*	Leviticus 11:29-30
LOCUST (Locust) *Shistocerca gregaria*	Judges 6:5; Exodus 10:19
MOUSE (House Mouse) *Mus musculus*	Leviticus 11:29-30
MOTH (Moth) *Microlepidoptera*	Isaiah 51:8
MULE (Mule) *Equus asinus mulus*	2 Samuel 18:9; 1 Kings 1:38
NIGHTHAWK (Kestrel) *Falco tinnunculus*	Leviticus 11:13-19
OSTRICH (Ostrich) *Struthio camelus*	Leviticus 11:13-19; Job 39:13
OWL (Long Eared Owl) *Asio otus*	Isaiah 34:11
PEACOCK (Common Peafowl) *Pavo cristatus*	1 Kings 10:22
PESTILENCE (Wasp) *Vespa orientalis*	Deuteronomy 7:20
PIG; BOAR (Wild Boar) *Sus scrofa.*	Leviticus 11:8; Luke 15:15
PIGEON (Rock Dove) *Columba livia*	Numbers 6:10
PURPLE (Murex) *Bulinus brandaris; Thais haemastoma*	Exodus 28:4-5; Esther 8:15
QUAIL (Quail) *Coturnix coturnix*	Numbers 11:31
RAM (Fat-tailed Sheep) *Ovis orientalis platyura*	Genesis 22:13; Exodus 29:32
RAVEN (Raven) *Corvus corone*	Genesis 8:7; Song of Songs 5:11
ROEBUCK (Fallow deer) *Dama dama*	Deuteronomy 14:4-6
SAND LIZARD (Skink) *Calcides; Scincus*	Leviticus 11:29-30
SCORPION (Scorpion) *Leiurus quinquestriatus*	Deuteronomy 8:15; Rev. 9:5
SEA GULL (Black Headed Gull) *Larus ridibundus*	Leviticus 11:13-19
SERPENT, ADDER (Palestinian Viper) *Vipera palaestinae*	Numbers 21:6; Proverbs 23:32
SHEEP (Fat-tailed Sheep) *Ovis orientalis platyura*	Exodus 22:30; Psalms 119:176
SILK (Silkworm) *Bombyx mori*	Revelation 18:12
SNAIL (Snail) *Helix*	Psalms 58:8
SNAKE (Crocodile) *Crocodilus niloticus*	Exodus 7:9; Isaiah 27:1
SPARROW (House Sparrow) *Passer domesticus*	Proverbs 26:2
SPIDER (Spider) *Araneae*	Isaiah 59:5-6;Job 8:14
STORK (Stork) *Ciconia ciconia*	Leviticus 11:13-19; Psalm 104:17
SWALLOW (Swift) *Apus apus*	Jeremiah 8:7
TURTLEDOVE (Turtle Dove) *Streptolepia turtur*	Numbers 6:10
VIPER (Cerastes Viper) *Cerastes cerastes*	Genesis 49:17;
VULTURE (Lappet-Faced Vulture) *Torgos tracheliotus*	Leviticus 11:13-19
WHATEVER HAS MANY FEET (Millipede) *Graphidostrepus syriacus*	Leviticus 11:41-42
WOLF (Wolf) *Canis lupus*	Genesis 49:27; Isaiah 65:25

Bibliography:

Animals and Plants of the Torah, (Hebrew), Feliks Y.,
Israel Zair Publishing House, 1993

Animals of the Bible, (Hebrew), Feliks Y., Sinai Publishing House, 1954

Animal Life in Biblical Lands, (Hebrew), Bialik Institute, 1956

Animals of the Bible, the Mishna and the Talmud,
(Hebrew), Grafor-Daftal Books, 1997

Illustrated Dictionary & Corcordance of the Bible, (English),
Macmillan Publishing House, 1986

Insight on the Scriptures, Volumes 1 + 2, (English), Watch Tower Bible
and Tract Society, 1988

The Complete Bible Handbook: An illustrated companion, (English),
Bowker J., Dorling Kindersley, 1998.

The Royal Purple & Biblical Blue, (English), Keter Publishing House, 1987